Prospero's Glove

Prospero's Glove

Poems by

Robert Edward Miss

Cover design by Shay Culligan

ISBN: 978-1-954353-40-4

Kelsay Books
502 South 1040 East, A-119
American Fork, Utah, 84003

Dedicated to my dear wife Judith Millman
who has encouraged my creativity in all kinds of ways
over many wonderful years together.

Acknowledgments

Thank you to these journals who initially published versions of the following pieces:

America Magazine: "Mythology at Fifty," (1996), "Good Friday 1964 Walking Westward" (1990)
Arc Westchester Side-by-Side Art/Poetry Festival: "Purple Rain"
Austin International Poetry Festival Anthology (2017): "Magnetic Poetry"
Crosswinds Poetry Journal (2018): "Snake Dance for Harrison"
Hudson Valley MOCA Writing the Walls (2018): "Amulets of Memory"

Many thanks also to Johnny Mattei for the cover art.

Contents

Prospero's Glove

(Magici Cambiamenti di Prospero)

Steel wheels rumble-thud across rusty rails.
Sparks flake into the darkling glen.
The night freight overtakes our garden
with awakening stealth.
Once again it passes unchallenged
through our dream-state
where troubles have sealed our fate.

Dear Prospero, we implore thee!
Wave your star-crusted glove.
Transform that moonlit galumpher.
Express us to Xanadu.
A crystal palace for our station,
a pleasure dome our destination.

Kamakura Americana

Nestling her back to me
Beneath enwrapping silk
Reveals only a naping upward
From gently rising shoulders
To an iridescent pitch of hair.

Her unguarded moments
Create a subtle-moving geometry
Like breeze-tossed lanterns
In an emperor's garden.
But I can feel the muted luminance
As a captured energy,
An inner Nippon beauty.

As I lift away the voile
To let my eye echo
Down her soft undulations,
A phantasmagorical scene slowly appears—
Blues, reds, and blacks
Invasively pigmenting her back.
Forming an Hiroshige,
Or perhaps Hokusai—
Those engulfing waves which could have
Heightened an evening's pleasure,
And that hovering crane
Summoning the imminence
Of a darkly-plumed husband,
Who will swoop home this morning
From some commercial conquest.

By purpose, she can no longer sleep
Immaculately sculpted to a lover's body.
Was there a vain hope
That this howling sea-artifice
Would replace the indelible horror
Of the Internment
When she was ten
And the government made its move
On the dangerous families of California?

This Nisei all-American,
Whose ingenuous chatter
Belies an experience
Of "the war at home,"
Must brittle-out
The day's first moments
Of camp-chill memories
And shake the shadow-fragments
Of father and mother
Whose hopes lie sharded
In the sands of Arizona.

Finding her worth today
In being duty-bound,
She will brim with consternation
When she awakens
To find the tingle of my scent
Permeating the stale serenity
Of her marriage.

But for now,
Her graceful slumber
Seeks out a sweet forgetfulness.
Her unrequited pain is stayed
By tenderness.

Sons of WWII

We hunched our backs and charged uphill. The knot
Of acid thrill which fired and drove us burst
The bowels, rammed the rib cage, jet-like shot
Us over hedge and ditch. Gun butts struck first.

We pounded hard until our arms were sore.
Above our battle cries a strange voice came.
One call quick-cooled the battle heat. The corps
Of gallant, sandlot warriors, stopped, turned tame.

"Oh, Jimmy, dinner time!" "Already?" "Now!"
With rifle, helmet Jimmy started home.
We bantered not of baseball games, but how
Marines were best, still bearing acid foam.

We bear it yet. We charge; we rage; we pound.
We aim our sterile guns at vacant ground.

From Arlington Cemetery

(December 1963)

John Kennedy's spirit
Presides peacefully at Arlington,
Because this valley of memorials
Exalts men like himself.
He asked nothing from his country,
But gave himself,
Spent and sealed in blood,
Witnessed by his country.

Crowds now witness the eternal flame,
A torch for our new generation.
All ages file past;
They pay their American tribute,
A simple but inscrutable do-what's-right,
Which really contains
Our majestic compassion
For our leader, our fallen son.

Amulets of Memory

A father and son push their six-foot seine
down Linganore Creek in the day's afterglow,
sloshing into the night.
Their prey are mad toms, those tiny catfish
that swim upstream when disturbed.
Good for bass bait in late summer
when the rivers are too clear to catch minnows.
The son, now grown and a Navy man,
is riding a River Patrol Boat
up the backwaters of the Mekong river,
watching for Viet Cong along muddy embankments
before night closes down and ground fire erupts.
Those Linganore nights
crouch in the back of his memory,
to be drawn out for comfort.
When thunder storms turn the Monocacy River
the color of tomato soup,
the run off from the Greenfield farms upriver,
fishing becomes impossible.
Father and son will shoot the riffles at Furnace Ford bridge,
drift under the stone aqueduct of the old C&O Canal,
marshalling into the clear expanse of the Potomac River
to fish for the day,
marveling at the occasional osprey
which plunges from a great height into the current
and emerges with a fish wriggling in its talons.
Amulets of memory afford this sailor a protective distance
from the muck and mayhem of the Mekong Delta.
He dreams of fishing once more on the rivers of his childhood.

Good Friday 1964 Walking Westward

John Donne in Central Park

Let a man's sphere be the path from Eighty-sixth
Around the bronzed Mad Hatter
Then back again.
Every turn affords fragmented bits of adolescent poetry:
The vagrants are dawdling elder statesmen;
The oaks are squirrel-worn to majestic cork palaces;
Children sail their boats with raucous dedication
        to Lewis Carroll;
And the weakened clack of Lenten sounds
Inside Ignatius Church
Implies the call of worshipful insects
Barely heard.
There goes a thoughtful man
Who thinks he's walking westward toward perpetual sunset—
His growing into Christ—a dying birth that may not end
Until he reaches the limpid vernal sun,
A pale medallion promising eternal summer.
He meanders, haunted by that muted Lenten clack,
A dull cry for Christ's mercy,
Which he teases, wrings and twists into a paean of joy.
But the slap of wood on wood holds an immutable resonance.
Emily Dickinson interrupts.
"Do you see God in a tree?
See Christ in a wide-eyed waif? Not me.
I see this elm and that pickaninny.
If love is a spark between two souls,
There Christ must be.
And who can see a spark except in the dark?
When life is bright and shiny,
We must turn it blithely between our fingers
Like a new penny."

Haiku Collection

Whisps of white smoke
Lick the chimneys and rooftops,
Tasting deep winter.

Red brambles bend down,
Ribs of barren wickiups,
Naked against the cold.

Rain patters the roof.
My pen inks notes for the day.
Clink, the coffee cup.

Above the black ridge,
a burnished archipelago
of scattered morning clouds.

Dawn's bank of fire-clouds
Silhouettes black-limbed trees;
My love and I watch.

Bird Walk

Her fleshy fingers primly held the small
Binoculars, five-power, Japanese.
She cried, "Look here!" All glasses focused; all
Matrons cooed, then sought our guide with pleas.

He drily told the markings, species, breed.
Then she expounded, taught the fledgling pair;
Her daughter Helen nodded, "yessed," agreed,
But pressed his hand. Eyes sang a mocking air.

She summoned George, her husband, lugging books,
Umbrella, charts. "The bird call, George." "You mean
The wooden whistle, dear?" With sideways looks
He rummaged round, soon dangled something green.

George jammed the books, the charts into his pack.
While Mother coaxed, he leered behind her back.

Dusk Flight

Zip, tick, flock of robins.
Claws click on silhouetted limbs,
Perched over the valley,
Spied through a pane turning to lead from loss of light,
A window in this mountain top studio.

In a bird's breath, they flick off,
The whole feathered band,
Higgledy piggledy throwing themselves
At the day's dying embers,
Western ridges of the Berkshires
Turning pink, orange, ruby, dusky rose.

Thrashing wildly but forcefully like blasted birdshot,
They fly southwest,
Seeking perpetual summer.

Orion Senex

From this mountain top studio,
The sky pitch-black long after midnight,
Orion's belt sparkles so close
That each star is a silver buckle
To be fiddled and undone.

But lady dawn imperceptibly begins her glide
Across the far horizon with calm certainty.
Constellations curtsey mildly,
Then fade with the retreating moon.

Gusts of wind animate the stubs of gnarled oaks,
While fleeting night ravages the rocks of their heat,
Signaling the chill of aborning day.

Soon the muffled rumble of the furnace below
Evokes warm memories of soft nudes
Fashioned here by smooth pastels
Swirling multicolored dust to the floor,
Remembering the years my artist's eye
Caressed the breasts of posing girls,
Their *pundendae* pulsating
With controlled excitement.

Those distant images linger
Until I spill coffee on the morning paper,
The cup unsteady in my gnarled and shaky hand.

Orange Humoresques

Sprock-et-ta. Sprock-et-ta.
Tik.
Sprock-et-ta. Sprock-et-ta.
Tak.
A petulant child
Huffing
Down the sidewalk
Hunching his back,
Clickety clack,
His stick ball bat
Pulled along the grillwork
Of Stuyvesant Park.

Watching that kid
Sucking an orange—
Remindful of Anna
Letting the tang
Steal through her mind,
Feeling the juice stream
Down her arm,
Watching those seeds
Drop to the cadence
Of a sultry afternoon.
Seed-upon-seed ticking to the sink
In her deep-dark kitchen
On a sultry afternoon.

Man from the Moon in My Hospital Room

This was not
just one of those things—
not a trip to the moon on gossamer wings—
not great fun ...
or a now and then fling.
This was serious sweat ... rapid pulse ...
throbbing head ... fetid breath ...
coming near death.
But then he appeared,
the quiet angel wearing patent leather shoes
with that look of bearing existential news ...
fat, somewhat homely,
resembling the son-in-law
of an old Jewish woman I knew.
His stubby fingers proffered a sheaf of pure white paper.
The pages shone brightly in the dim night light
as he pushed them towards me.
No printing, no fancy calligraphy,
just clean, square sheets of alabaster.
Is this where I begin the beguine, turn a new leaf?
Am I free to recover, endure this pain and get better?
I looked down at my book to mark the place,
looked back to see his face.
He had disappeared with the gift
that brought him here.
But mysteriously a new idea came floating
through the hospital's septic atmosphere.
"Questi non cibera terra ne peltro,
ma sapienza, amore e virtute."
He will not feed on land or money,
but on wisdom, love and valor ...
I received this thought from Dante,
his gift to lift my heart from this *Inferno*.

Captain of the Universe

I wanted to be Captain of the Universe,
Wear golden cuff links spewing starbursts,
Scintillas lighting up the night,
My silver Harley streaking sparks on dark country roads.
I wanted the magic power to create mysteries,
Like two headed buffalos on the western plains
Or camels born twin-Siamese on the Sahara dunes.
I'd make them run in two directions at once,
Spinning out of control, whirling dervishes of the wild.
From such magical miracles the Cree and Shoshones could
Break free of enslaving drugs and government.
The nomads could create a new religion,
One of peace and majesty.
We could fill rodeo side shows and the temples of the East.
Have all the people in this creaking world
Flock, marvel and pray.
Instead, I made a web site to demonstrate my powers,
While setting traps for secret agents who were following me.
Like most laymen, they don't understand the secret meanings
Of time-traveling the galaxies,
Nor can they decipher the tapping of dolphins on the hulls
Of Navy submarines surging toward secret destinations.
People only focus on what is.
Or hear only the daily noise and news.
As Captain of the Universe I could have inspired them.
But I burnt out in a streak of glory,
Brandishing my AK47,
Riding side-saddle on my bike.
I ended by driving in opposite directions,
Spinning like a *darling whervish*
Into Bliss.

The Man with No Name

She never called him by his name.
Someone, not her, had invited him to join the household.
This man with no name was a wispy, warm presence,
always keeping his place, mostly out of sight,
except when he got drunk one Christmas night
and tried to give every child a fresh clean twenty-dollar bill,
chasing each of them gleefully around the dining room table.
This made them love him more and her less, she thought,
standing as she would in the doorway,
her arms folded tight against her bosom.

The turtle dove proclaimed his elegant name
throughout the land as a descendent of kings,
but it was muffled by a dull silence hanging
in the dim dining room air,
disallowing an epiphany.

The English could have dubbed him Emanon,
just as they changed all the names in Ireland,
disenfranchising the people
who could no longer recognize
their very own pathways and places.
But their cherished poesy would not die,
and neither that sly look playing upon their faces.

Withholding a name can
diminish the other to silent observer,
but cannot change the whispered secrets
between two lovers or impede
the natural love of honest children.

Benedict Pond

At first light, I walk from my cabin
into the raw reality of natural beauty,
up the Appalachian trail toward Benedict Pond,
seeking solitude with a mix of apprehension and desire.
Maybe the wild dogs will be patrolling there …
Maybe not.

Deep into my soul I tiptoe a log path
snaking through a patch of swamp,
a painfully slow endeavor as
I watch for flashing fangs in every step,
six bushy tails lowered for the lunge.

Rather than a pack of beasts to do me harm,
I find a perfect circle burnt into the ground.
Above the blackened earth without a sound
a thousand fireflies abandoned by the night
create a charming infestation.

One lands nimbly on my arm as if to welcome me.
I soften into neither the hunted nor the hunter
but another choice,
an alignment with the inner voice of the universe,
the message I had been seeking at Benedict Pond
year after year with all my might,
captured in this winged oracle's tiny pulse of light.

Benedict Pond, twice I circle round
in exultant celebration before heading home
while gradually a poignant meaning seeps into my ken.
This vaginal shape of steel-toned water,
cold and remote,
nestled in the verdant earth,

my incessant destination,
signifies my distanced mother,
and my desperate need for affection.
As I start back, a chattering nuthatch
greets me,
not two feet away,
hanging upside down from a trailside birch.
She doesn't scold me like a jay,
but her staccato notes seem to say,
give yourself to what is with a gentle joy.

Snake Dance for Harrison

One bright day while the thunder god *Haokah*
boomed over the Navajo wedding blanket
of your ancestors, the vision of you was born
through the long snake dance
that brings a warrior for peace
into our dream world of blue sky and purple flowers.

As you do know, you will shed your skin many times
to become the soft-spoken, brave new man
who will make your mother, your father,
and your elders proud.

Let your heart be your kiva where a vision of your
very own world emerges.

Let your hands clap twice three magic times,
one, two, three.
Let your feet stomp twice three powerful beats,
one, two, three.
Let your spirit reach for the sun many times
to guide you on every quest.

You are the one who makes the blazing sky
smile upon us. You are the one who makes us bend
to kiss the dew-drop flowers.

You will be one of the ones to lead our human race.
We can divine it in your face.
Thank you, Little Brother. Amen.

A Catfish Secret

A catfish breaks water
Pretending to be a bass,
Hooked all the same.
What does a catfish eat?
What's his most favorite treat?
Something that comes in a can.
Cut up little squares of Spam.
Wham!
I think I hooked a big one.

Dreamscape

Bright moon at pre-dawn,
sweet cacophony of birds.
I dreamt you were here.
Did you whisk past
into the vaulted chamber,
or did you embrace me naked
in the moss green shade?
I can't remember.

Chet

He was standing on a rock
Staring into the deep woods
When we met.
Stretching out his mocha hand,
He said, "I'm Chet."
A cold voice whispered to me,
"This Chet survived Attica."
Acrid smoke, shouts and gunshots
Flashed through my core while I asked inane
First-blush questions.
We walked up the mountainside conversing.
At the trail head I rummaged in my pouch,
Pulled out a carefully stashed johnnycake,
Broke it and held half out to him,
"Take this and eat,
It's the best thing you will ever have."
Hesitant at first, he opened his fist,
Received it and raised his hand to take a bite,
Thus revealing these numbers on his wrist,
9–13–71, that was the last day of the riot.

Chet Revista

I turned around and there he was,
Coming through the arch of platform thirty-two.
He moved with an imperial stride towards
The big clock of Grand Central Station,
Seeming circumspect and distant,
Just like our first meeting on that mountain trail.
While we had verbally circled each other
In a respectful exchange,
A wild and surreal intuition took hold of me,
Filling my psyche with acrid smoke, shouts and gunfire.
Amidst this confusion a still small voice whispered,
"He survived the Attica riots."
No trail khakis and boots this time,
But dashikis, he and his six tall followers.
Shiny purples laced with golden threads,
Brocaded mantles of deep maroon.
Lizard-green kufis all around.
Chet glided past, no turn in my direction.
Another sudden insight—
I craved his self-revelation to the Attica fight,
Thus allowing me self-indulgent compassion.
Such was not to pass as he led
Up the promenade and out-of-sight,
A potentate of the night.

My Bodhisattva Attendant

Storming out of the woods and up a fire trail,
A figure on the hill attended my arrival,
But disappeared.
My greeter was either a vanishing woodland spirit
Or that burned out stump fronded by a dwarf Ailanthus.
Alone in a dark wood,
My mind often composes a human shape
From mere shadows and windblown limbs.
What did appear trailside was the grey hump-backed boulder
Where I first met Chester.
He was perched on top, staring into the ravine below.
His mocha complexion melded into the woods.
His Buddha belly was evident under his khaki shirt.
A walking stick with its carved lion handle
Balanced his stance.
He seemed to be in a meditative trance.
As I hoisted myself atop the boulder,
An eerie feeling came over me.
"Chester is dead," whispered an inner voice.
We had always engaged in the bland conversations
Of acquaintances meeting randomly in strange places.
But this mysterious man in the scruffy hiking shoes,
Whenever I met him on the trail,
Magically infused me
With life-affirming feelings.
I never learned his true identity,
But consistently felt his energy.
Chester, my soul told me, has moved
To his next assignment,
Guardian of this vast forest and the paths
That lead to safety,
A modern *bodhisattva attendant*
Who will protect this green from evil devastation.

Hovering Angel

A Reflection about Darcy

We were sitting at a table in Neil's Coffee Shop,
corner of Seventy and Lex.
I thought the subway underneath
was making the building shake.
I found out later it was the Hovering Angel, mad as hell.
Darcy had wrestled him all night long until daybreak.
It was a standoff, as it had been for many months.
I had rushed uptown when she rang my office,
the cubicle where I was eking out a living,
fighting off my own demons, but nothing like her
life and death struggle down in Durham.
Looking back, there was a strange vibration going on,
but I was unaware, happy to see my old friend.
It had been many years,
but our relationship had been so warm and personal,
it never faded. We talked all morning.
For Darcy, New York was a stopover on her way to Europe,
just her and her husband. Not the kids.
That should have been a tip off.
This would be her last trip before the final passage.
We talked of our days at Carolina.
I first met her in a television course.
Very pregnant with her second child,
I helped her down gently from a steel ladder
where she had nonchalantly adjusted a fresnel studio light.
After grad school, we would meet
at the Carolina Coffee Shop for long talks
about almost anything, politics, family,
but mostly art, movies, opera, poetry.
She was my connection to a cultural world
I had little time for. Sarcastically I now referred to myself
as the "mogul," managing a television studio, ambitious.

Darcy was not a good looker,
but an old soul of joyful sensuality
balanced by a stern practicality,
a trait she adopted as a teenager
working in the garment district.
We were never physical friends,
but her mere touch on my shoulder warmed my heart.
Like the day we took a long walk in Duke Gardens.
She had read my experimental television play.
No one else who mattered to me seemed to get it.
Darcy in her unfailing creative sense
nailed it immediately.
"This is really a libretto for a rock opera."
I have never forgotten that day. She legitimatized my work
as only a revered friend can do.
Now we were in a venerable old New York City coffee shop,
not unlike the one in Chapel Hill,
observing how sexy
Monteverdi's *L'incoronazione di Poppea* could be.
She was hoping to see a production of it in Paris
the following week. I hope she did.

Woman in a Silver Frame

Weeping, pleading to be heard,
but not a word escaped
the disembodied head of a woman
floating in the pitch black hole
above the theater lighting grid.

That night a muffled scratching
against a distant door
I'm sure was my friend,
snatched from life,
trying to return from the dead.

In the broad of day, a *shiva* call,
an old picture of a young woman
stood on the mantle.
A warm smile in black and white,
framed in chilling silver.

I turned away to cry when I saw it;
no one was watching.
I remember the cherry petals flying off
the rooftop of the hearse as it drove away.
Her soul was free.

Eagle Hill

A Reflection

Seated on a granite bench,
framed by mountain laurel all abloom,
I had tuned out the honks and the barks
floating from the valley below,
when an exotic man
hiking up the steepest side of the peak
interrupted my reverie.
Forging a straight line through the underbrush,
his curiously carved walking stick stabbed the ground
with each definitive step.
A trace of a smile crossed his leathery face
as he gave me a sign of peace
before disappearing back down the hill,
the one I had run up, straight up, many times
to test my "readiness"
when I ran marathons and trail races.
I am now content to walk,
choosing twisted rocky paths
where natural details open up to observe and savor,
like the young deer so close I could see the suede nap
of his juvenile horns.

Today my walk took me down Sleepy Hollow trail,
across Pocantico River, no more than a creek,
then up the steep climb to the view from Eagle Hill.
The trail runs along a rough wall
of lichen-patched boulders,
bordered by rotting old fence posts
and rusted strands of wire.

These are the remnants of a long abandoned farm.
Beyond the wall were sprouts of skunk cabbage,
chartreuse leaves amidst the remains
of a late snowfall in early spring.

I knew in my mind's eye that back a narrow
path into that scraggly woods sits a boulder all alone,
the size of a house, a so-called "erratic"
deposited there by an ancient glacier.

As sure as I'll return
to the bosom of Abraham,
I know Indians gathered
at that massive rock
where a leathery-faced medicine man
would lift his carved spirit stick
in a sign of peace and pour out
supplications to the Great Father.
There would be fervent dancing
in celebration around the sacred stone
under shadowy moonlight.
I will hike back that path when I can,
and stand for a spell in respectful silence.

Blackbird Greeting

A low-flying vermillion patch
on a pitch-black wing cuts my path.
Seconds behind, a burst of gold on tiny wings.
The goldfinch disappears,
but the red-winged blackbird
watches from a nearby branch.
We seem to fix each other's gaze
before I take a lakeside bench
to enjoy islands of water lilies.
They rise and fall
in the wake of paddling ducks.
Not six feet from where I sit
a song erupts from water's edge.
My red-winged greeter has landed here.
Peeking through a leafy sassafras,
his familiar splattering rasp
punctuates each flute-like phrase.
Soon his serenade abruptly ends
as he decorously takes flight.

Walking back,
a mere four paces up the trail,
a jazzy catbird dances in the dirt.
He shows off his chestnut rump
then flits through the underbrush.
Today I walked slow to my woodland haunts.
A tick-borne germ had kept me weak
and long at home.
Perhaps my natural friends conspired
to celebrate my surprise return.

A Fibonacci of Birds

The woods are entombed
in a late winter silence.
No wind, a motionless sea of dead leaves
with no verdant underbrush.
An empty solitude like a church on Holy Saturday.
Suddenly a woodpecker's squawk
from the summit of a naked oak
crashes the mood.
Each screech is punctuated by a rata tat tat,
over and over.
Then a double staccato beat.
Rata tat tat.… tat rata tat. A percussive Palestrina.
Two large "red-headers,"
heard from their loft, but unseen.
Three nuthatches join the rhythm,
cavorting playfully around the trunk of a maple tree.
Hatches like to tweak the bark upside down.
Sometimes a pair. Seldom three.
At the bottom of the trail,
five mallards paddle around the rocks
of a frothy brook.
Four drakes and a hen.
She endlessly chases her favorite, again and again.
A Fibonacci of birds.
But where are the eight feathered something else?
Too early for crows to head home to roost.
No high-flying flocks of Canada geese.
As I near a clumpy patch of swamp,
I hear a chorus of peepers pre-cursing spring.
Many more than eight, maybe eight hundred.

So much for an avian Fibonacci,
shifting now to amphibians.
We can impose our human order on things,
but nature holds a multitude of slippery numbers.

Backwash

Each year the river swells below and stops
This stream. By stealth the river sends its wake,
Not force. It creeps, invades dirt roads and crops.
Low torrent then becomes a ribbon lake.

In spring, red rolling mud, a seething soup
Boils down, engulfs rapids, island, pier,
But this gray seep, strange backwash flood, takes stoop
And sill off guard, strikes up a fancy-fear.

We snake through treetops, stubble rooted deep.
Now, far above the heel-packed lovers' path
The stagnant stream we boat would seem to keep
Some secret force beneath, some hidden wrath.

Although we talk and laugh, for just a space
I catch a touch of fear upon Ann's face.

After the Storm

My morning star,
a most gentle priestess,
anoints each snow-bound limb
outside my window.
She plies her soft ritual
slowly through the predawn light.
Now my new day of crystalline air
will blank the terror of black night's
winter maelstrom.

Flying with Bettie Page

I'm trapped in a somber mood,
until Bettie Page appears against the sky,
stretched facedown across the wing of a diving biplane.
Her red shorts and black halter give me a thrill.
She winks.
The plane climbs straight up until she slips into thin air.
I gasp in fear.
That sly little wink made me care.

Magnetic Poetry

from word pieces on a magnetic board

universe of lightning
bloom of language
happy animal remembers

holiday thought
winter season
garden watch

green summer shine
picnic dream cycle
beautiful promises

rain hard
change through flowers

dance more
celebrate always
give soft love this year

Coming Upon the Egyptian Curtain

It startled me like an awakened baby
As I rounded the corner
To the darkened alcove where it stood.
I broke into tears.
The compact and luminous focus,
Bounded by unrelenting black
Had the effect of an emotional laser beam.

The foreground curtain of those exotic loops
And leafy patterns most loved by Matisse
Imposed a surprising depth-of-field in a small space.
The light through the window framing a palm tree canopy
Imparted a glow to the bowl of pomegranates
On the table below.
What is it about Henri's Interior with an Egyptian Curtain
That draws one so intimately into this well-defined,
Calm and color-fast world?

Geraldo Contemplates

I know you're there, seated on an azure blue chair.
After all, you're an artist, a rainbow master.
You're inside the painting but not of it.
Out of sight, but I see you.
You light up a cigarette,
The brand that killed you.
In your thoughtful manner that I best remember,
You consider the patterns of the Egyptian curtain.
You run your imagination
Over the fertile pomegranate shapes.
You relish the play of colors,
The pale blue fruit bowl
On the pink cloth
By the sunlit window.
Your own being is slyly absorbed into the black borders,
But I know you're there.
I'm your brother, blood of your blood,
That dried up and blew out the window
Of Johns Hopkins Cancer Care.
That was the day you danced into dark
Embraced by your lady love.
So light up now, enjoy haunting this creation.
Invade Matisse as you wish.
Inhale the chromatics of eternal contemplation.

November Sun

Bare light through barren branches,
This sun warms only through windows.
Crystal air is winter's passion.
This faint light
Warms through delicate glass
Long-seasoned lovers,
Each other's blazing prism
Whatever the solstice.

Thoughts from the Commuter Bus:

Snow in the Salt Grasses
The salt grasses, greedy tassels,
Catch the snow
And are bowed over.

Snow in the Barberries
This crusty old city
Pulls us past her turnpike's
Snow-flecked barberry bushes.
We slide into her thorny tunnel
Searching for morning coffee.

Winter Light

We swam through subterranean streams,
Both encountering milk-white eels,
Whose teeth fell away from their bloodied mouths.

Then mysteriously together
We rose for air
To find an amber crater lake,
A palisaded star-pool under the chilling sky.

Miraculously we became two skimming birds
Above the licking surface,
Yearning toward a westward glow—
A roseate winter's light,
Through our own quartz-like
Limitless air.

For Julie

Come, dance on the grave
Of my old self with me.

Sew petals where the stone
Ultimately will be.

And try to see
This ethereal, practical
Future all about us.

As we strut down the boulevards …

Striking our poses,
Stroking each other,
Strewing our roses.

Come, dance our dance with me,
Making it up as we go.

Singing our song
To this lopsided world,
And each other.

Overpeck Park One Summer Sunday Evening

Trees dot the landscape toward infinity
Like a Renaissance vision of heaven.
Lovers' bubbling laughter catches in the branches,
Then flies for the boundless sky.
Jamaicans play cricket at a distance,
Ghostly in their whites.
Runners flit along the paths,
Seeming to disappear into the languid air.
And strollers
Have positioned themselves perfectly
For the painter's eye.
Did God make this?
Or was this conceived by man?

Overpeck Park One Winter Sunday Morning

Trees spread their spikey branches
Towards the grayness
Like anemones
Yearning for surface light
And the nurturing particles it sends.
Two runners float past each other
Without a sound.
The park is deserted. The gulls are in charge.
There's your answer.

With Judith at Lauderdale

Our green-foamed beach grades
To the world's blue curve
Dancing on its sand-blown waves
Its many mixturing shades—
Daring every fisherman's nerve
To hang flags
And drop nets
On that far out horizon.

We are safer here.
But there's daring
In that energy between us.
The curve of your back
Mixing in the green black
Of my shade.
Promises kept
Equaling promises made.

The Moon Slipper

The moon slipper forever falls
Beneath the seabed.

A Duet

I know not how to trace
My fancy's wisps or thighs
Upon this paper:
This fitting persons to planes,
Stacking syllables to sheets—
Collated whisperings.

Who could document the soundless landscape
Where we meet?
If time is space,
There is no calculus of hour or place
In our equation.

~

When we watch the downys,
The hairys, the hatches
Flit beyond the glass,
Our patch of quiet,
A swatch of some large bolt,
Wraps 'round us,
But brings the chill
Of setting out one's suit
For high occasion.
Nothing's happening:
That's the good news.
Something's about to:
That's destiny.
The quiet pause is not
A sum of each,
But us.
While beyond the glass,
The downys, the hairys,
The hatches fuss.

Gardenia Song

It was a balmy night
Of shiny leaves
Of moistened lips,
And a bright gardenia in your hair.

You said it reminded you of a past affair,
But I didn't care,
If that brought you where
We love-locked
And fell to the ground.

I caught ecstasy in your face
When a trace of the flower's
White fragrance filled our embrace.

The only sound
On that hushed hot night
Was the hum of our bodies
Making love again and again.

To Catch a Thief

My mind can see
Our Rolls winding maniacally
Down hairpin turns towards the
Ultimate shore.

Is it southern France?
An isle of the Peloponnese?
To Catch a Thief?
Are you my companion Princess Grace?

Our bodies fly through
Trees on magnetic beams
Seeking targets which are ourselves
While the car descends.

How marvelous to see
The glamorous context of our lives
At this burning sweet moment.

When we join the Rolls
As it sluggishly roils
Towards the spreading beach,
We'll take the bitter with the sweet
Once again.

Purple Rain

Lost in the land of purple rain,
Trying to find my life again.
An old friend meets me one sad day
Who patiently helps me understand
How to be happy in this purple land.
How friends heal friends along the way

The Wild Boys of Schoolhouse Road

Three overalled cousins I had never met
Stood with arms folded.
Politely they challenged me to a race
Across the open field. How dare they!
Me who had commanded
Expeditionary forces of lead soldiers,
Managed fleets of cast iron trucks,
The province of an only child.
As they stared at me, an electric shiver
Triggered my jump out front
Before they could take off.
Never before had I felt such acceleration.
Never before had I sucked wind so hard my stomach hurt.
The veins in my neck were throbbing as I kept the lead,
But they were gaining on me.
We raced across corn stubble to a crooked creek
Gouging through the topsoil.
Those three scruffians passed me
And stopped dead.
With iridescent snot hanging from his nose
One cousin was pointing into the creek.
I thought he saw a snake, a big chub, or maybe a muskrat.
No. It was the clay bottom laid out
In sweeping layers of muted rainbow colors.
As if respectfully showing a visitor from the orient,
They proudly stood there letting me marvel at the
Striations of copper, silver, pale green and coral.
We walked quietly back to the farm house—united somehow
By the beauty of what we saw.

Birthday Surprise

I swung from musty shadows
Onto the milk-skinned bridge butter-scotched
With the morning sun,
A concrete ridge hunching
Over a green sea-to-become stream
And huddling beneath an azured forever
That drew my arms wonder-wide and tingling.
But what was that jingling?
A lone, somehow familiar stranger
Was shuffling away with age-measured insistence,
A figure from somewhere in my existence.
Would I recognize his face?
The question shot me into race with curiosity.
Long loafer strides hopscotching pavement cracks
Bounced me green to blue, blue to green
Until sky and stream whorled
About the unconcerned shuffler,
Scuffling his beeline towards some dreamed destination.
His crumpled fedora like the bashed in butt of a joke
Showed more than elbow knocks with laughter.
His worn brown sun-drunken coat
Warmly radiated a grandfather of a thousand places.
I tiptoed behind him hope-tensed to see a friend
Beyond the bend of his back.
He seemed stooped in wonder at the dust he stirred,
Which added to the dust of wander on his shoes,
Like a Jew's.
At the tug of a coat sleeve he halted,
But only my fingers planted in his shoulder
Gently pulled him round.
My hand dropped back to its place
            When he stared down with that face—
                  The face of a sad clown.

A Motle

When in the southern sun of boyhood
I caught lightly in my fingers
A butterfly black and dappled;
With fascination, infatuation, I pulled
Apart each velvet segment
To find its mystery.
Tearfully I found in the tearing
The secret had fluttered
And gone.
I later learned to share their sun,
And the mystery was mine.

Despair of a Southern Officer

At the surrender of Lee
A recurrent glint of patrilineal steel
Slashed the moss-hung cypress shade.
The distended veins of a scream
Heard only in the heart,
The lye-sear of tearless anger,
And a twisting urgency to tear out
The charred remnants of my innocence and hope
Had burst into a veering-to-death dance,
When suddenly a chill pierced my flaring shoulders.
Out beyond the craze of shadows stood a stripling,
Poised, unafraid.
The sun crowning his hair played
Darkness over his face. His shy tracings
In the sand somehow mocked
My blush of naked frenzy. I lurched forward,
Offered the sword's hilt that the glitter
Of its gilded heritage might
Excite wonder and wide eyes.
But he paused for just the breadth of a knowing smile,
Like a rusted peddler's I had someplace seen,
Or dreamed.
In a tick then, he flicked off through the marshes,
Left me standing there, burnished by sunlight,
Where laughter crowned my tears
With trembling new life.

When I Walk at Night between Nickelodeon Days

When I walk at night towards
Our old country house, its saffron lamps
Seem to inhale, exhale softly
The sweet ether.
Pliable leaves underfoot add
A distance to the day's
Rinky dink patterns.
Now, at last, we can let go!
The world won't rollaway and
Run bumpity, bump, crash
Into a hedgerow.
Tonight …
Stars in the oaks, breeze through the pines,
The chiffon presence of shad bush and quince.
Breathe in … slowly …
Breathe out.
Yes, we'll have to put another nickel in,
But that's tomorrow.

Message from Jonah

Rivers and rows of fields,
All the low places,
Find their inevitable western edge
To be the morning's glowing,
Cleanly golden frontier.

Pass through these burnished extremities.
Race toward each fleeting sunlit epiphany.
But prepare!
To be swallowed into dark!
By twilight's red cirrus monsters!

Fiddlers' Convention

The acorn hangs on,
One tick from the plummet.
So the galaxy,
And so Galax, Virginia.

Keep fiddling, boys.
Don't count on that oak
Or a falling star
For your mighty new world.
Just play on.

Nightwalking Your Champagne Poodle

When your poodle turns to Wolfman,
His canines gleam in moonlight.
When champagne turns to silver,
Walk by his side toward daylight.

If you slip beyond his footfall,
He will down you at the oak tree.
Keep your stride an easy measure.
When you reach the porch,
You're home free.

Looking Back on Pleasure Island

We stepped lightly through
The hip-high grass as soon as the
Punt crunched the sandbar,
Then penetrated the island, a dark mound
Dwarfed by its disproportionate maples
Brushed silver with rhythmic breezes.
Then spread our Peruvian blanket
As a fiery inset to the brown surround,
Allowing our well-sunned bodies
To complete a languid mosaic.
A creek willow gently nudged
Up and down, up and down in the river current.
A basket (appropriately packed with wine and cheeses)
Held in a hidden pouch
A golden chain!
Over your head with a smile,
It fell upon your breasts.
The chain is lifted,
Each tender nipple kissed,
I run my hand down across
A pelvic territory created to be touched,
Then both hands up through all your arched topography.
Down and up the willow in the water.
Deftly—as I remember—a kiss is placed
In the small of your back.
Your trilling laughter seemed to attract
The flight of scarlet birds on black wings.
Your arms around my neck pulled us over.
Our mutual mouths at once contained
Two writhing denizens—like a fish in-hand underwater.
The creek willow up and down.
Titters of scarlet all about.
Then only silence and slow, silver motion ...

I am watching now the soundless circling of an osprey
As I stretch backward in the shallows of a sandbar.
Your earth and nectar fragrances still enveloping me
Are released to the air by the eddying currents.
I ask the osprey—keen observer of all that went before—
"Will I ever see her again?"
Is his distant, voiceless answer a kind of
"Nevermore?"

Mythology at Fifty

Like a fable of an ancient age,
A plunge into a darkened glade
Is etched upon my boyhood frieze
Of memories.

It was a twilighted summer evening
After an Olympic-bolted storm.
The bizarre sky was lurid
Against the lush woods, deep green and still.
The soaked, black earth
Exuded a primal river smell
Mixed with the grassy fragrances
One never forgets.

A trail's entry
Into the dripping veil of trees
Was like an open-mouthed nature god
Whose lizard tongue
Might flash-curl me
Into its awesome mysteries.

What a difference now—
From being that golden lad,
Robust but primordially fearful,
To becoming a young man
Searching for his virility
And having it all the time,
To the young adult, savvy and sexy
Without knowing it,
To the caring father
Who then evolved
Into a leader of soft-leather words and deeds.

Toko-Ri

Silverados
On shadberry trails
And breaking waves.
Sky blue herons
Swoop spinnaker sails
And drowning rays.

Black-bottom jetties
Tell sandcastle tales
To the hungry sea.

Faint rosie cliffs
Spurn whalers' pleas,
La da da, dee dee dee.

Two hundred years on down the line,
Will our fleeting fish have gone?
What beast will eat our swimmers
Just for fun?

You can't get back to Toko-Ri, my friend,
Once the bridge is out at Toko-Ri.

Plankton Follies

Strands of rubious sea kelp
Lie beached ajumble,
Ready to pull
Anyone of fearful imagination
Into its muscular roots and tendrils.
Gusts of sting-rain
Prickle nerve endings
Tuned squint-ward
Towards yonder whale spouts.
Their spray arches nano seconds
Above wave surges
Scrolling the ebbed cove,
Gem-smoothing a-froth
This scattered Stonehenge
Of mega boulders,
Scavenging every ort that can feed
A hungry sea.
The jet-flip of a tail!
Or not?
Are they vaulting
Amid the electro-kinetics
Of choppy currents?
Or just laying out there bemused
By this solitary prurient?
A shaman's swirl of misty rain
Reveals a craggy gateway
Leading to another fissure
And thoughts tinctured
With arcane possibilities.
And behold! A darkened tunnel
Pouring from the looming face
Of a Gibraltar-stone
Contemplating Asia.

A passage carved before migrations
Of any legged thing,
Seeming to echo through its dampened walls
A sea beast's incantation,
"Enter here, if you dare."
Like an I Ching throw
It tenses the heart.
But aren't those offshore beings
Merely chanting humorously
At this silly exploration,
Plankton sluicing their smile-cocked mouths,
Fulminating something known but not admitted—
That the Soul makes its own mysteries
At its own times?

Cybele

Black trees,
Winter snow,
A color-undulating rainbow
Dilating through me and beaming the woods,
Swirling the house.
My harmonics, my song to the universe,
A clue to "what-is."

On your windowsill framing this view—
Fourteen glass paperweights
Arranged in progressive hue
By subtle degrees of the spectrum.

You naturally knew what only now I know—
I had seen that ancient wisdom
In your girl of an early photograph—
The wise old young Cybele.

The truth of the black trees;
The beauty of the snow—
Waiting for the story that I'll tell.
The colors are in the tolling,
Not the bell.

Our Island Goddess *Hitanacha*

We recklessly swam
Her spring flood
In our boy-bodies,
Regarding slithering vortexes
She created to swallow us.
We dove from my square-ended launch
Held shivering fast by anchor ropes.
They were strumming "someone's in the kitchen with Dinah"
While *Hitanacha's* silt mound
Rose calmly above the river churn-up.

She would sweep us downstream,
Me and my comrades, gawking
At her green cascades of creek willows
And thickets of scrubby bushes,
All spread-leg defiant
Against a turbulent sky.

In July, wind-starts
Would complacently shimmer silver
Through her island maples.
But the mud and musk scent
Of her cool, secret shade
Stuck to us boys,
Lingering even as we waded barefoot in the shallows
Of the sparkle and bubble of her sandbars.
Afternoon storm clouds loomed behind us
And mothers downstream
Rightfully wondered our whereabouts.
And we higgledy-piggledy whistled and burbled
On our search for mussels, chub and dace,
While *Hitanacha* breathed her call to manhood
Across each spell-bound face.

In swarmy August,
We worked our spinners
For deep-pooled bass.
As our boat surged the riffles,
Our mind-tongues ran up and down
The pulchritude of next year's class.
And when our dream-glide of fantasy girls
Moved past *Hitanacha's* entreating glade,
We lured them inside for our love-act charade.

I visit her now in my Autumn age.
She's smaller than remembered,
But the old rage against the sky
Remains in her outstretched branches.
October's clearwater is slow calm,
Allowing time to remember those summers
When each dragonfly gave her a nipple kiss,
Every mad tom and swimmer-beast
Professed her deity.

From her flickering shadows now,
A reverent blue heron
Watches the shallows
For a feast.
There's mournful hope
In his stance,
His Ming vase dance
On her tattered shoreline.

Scherzo for the Loogaroo*

Juana, the exiled Cuban pianist runs her fingers over
a Chopin Scherzo with focused rage.
At the Colon in Buenos Aires, they raved.
Carnegie Hall, New York, the *Anglos* stood and cheered.
Yet her long-bridled hopes for a free Cuba
fill this salon performance with bristling *ex-patria* feelings.
The audience of docile sophisticates
seated on folding chairs with folded hands
misconstrues each frenetic arpeggio
to be a devil-dance for Chopin.

But it's Juana exorcising her demons.
Unseen are her seething shape-shiftings
where her arms stretch longer and longer
away from the keyboard
as she grabs each articulated chord.

Once smoldering grief now catches flame
and begins melting her into the floor
as her very own *Loogaroo,*
unobserved by the crowds
streaming through the dark streets below,
appears chillingly at the apartment window.

Silhouetted through flaming curtains,
his misshapen extremities engulf Juana
in a passionate embrace.
Then with a muffled flutter, they disappear
on leathery wings as the piano continues
into the final movement

and flourishes to the finish.
After mild applause, the audience dissolves
into a sweet summer evening
of housekeeping natterings and critical sighs.

A mythological vampire of the Caribbean

Gambrill Mountain

I loved her—my Gambrill Mountain.
I was drawn to her like a child snuggling
into his mother's bosom.
I feared her—my mother mountain.
A fear so strong I climbed up her
laurelled ravines looking side-to-side,
ahead and behind,
as if a headless mistress of death
might take me by surprise,
or a powerful force would enthrall
me to be chained forever to a wall
somewhere in her limestone caverns.
Then one day I found an ancient rifle
in my uncle's closet.
Single action, twenty-two caliber,
monstrously tarnished but workable.
He let me have it, an indulgent gift
for my tender twelve years.
With a handful of shells, hollow points,
I crossed the road onto one of her paths,
expecting my own hollow feelings and fears,
but I was drawn to the brightening abundance
of those tiny green leaves of spring
and the translucent clusters
of terrapin eggs uncovered by April rains.
To my surprise, gun slung over my arm,
behind not one tree was there a shadowy foreboding
to haunt me. I felt mysteriously free.
That rifle became my boon companion
over many trails, many treks for many miles.
I never fired it once. It never let me down.
My mountain mother and I enjoyed each other
in a peace profound.

Copperhead Reveries

A fanciful rumor of copperheads hanging
from the rafters of an abandoned cabin,
discovered by a game warden, now deranged,
was the magnet that drew me up Rocky Springs hollow,
past the backwoods lodge where Hood College girls rode
their dutiful horses for an overnight stay.
I fantasized about them briefly,
but a nest of snakes flourishing in a wasted cabin
was the draught of curiosity laced with fear
I wanted to taste.

I wandered through mountain laurel,
circumventing fire ponds and ant mounds,
discovering an occasional box turtle,
a black racer gliding over warm rocks,
the whispering flight of a great horned owl
rarely seen in daylight.
But no copperheads in sight.

Every night now I become
the legendary game warden
who enters that derelict shack
only to be engulfed by snakes
lurching from above,
undulating across floorboards,
slithering over my boots
with their ornate pattern
of a lover's glove.

I back out the door
and pell mell crash down the mountain
scratched and bruised by the underbrush,
past tethered horses snorting nervously,

then plunge through a darkened door
to be surrounded
by gyrating limbs and breasts,
naked women sprawled in the dark.
I strain my eyes to be sure.
But memory fades before …
I awake.

Bungalow Boy

A Great Horned Owl peeked in my window.
I rode his back across the woods,
up and down the river
looking for my mother.
The moon was bright enough but
he couldn't go beyond the pine trees,
his territory. She wasn't anywhere.

A red fox darts across the road.
I can feel the morning dew between my toes
as I walk around the house.
A pigeon hawk is circling,
the mockingbird gives warning;
My Mom knows a lot about birds.

Looking down the road, where is she?
I run my foot back and forth
along the porch boards,
gray paint flakes off into the grass.
Not much to do here except run around the yard
with my brother and sister.
They're still asleep in the back room.
My dad's Harley is hidden in the tobacco barn.
His friend brought us here.
I miss my Mom.

Stone Walls and Solitude

Did she think something was wrong with me,
musing to her sister Marie as they thumbed
through the Spiegel's catalogue on a Sunday afternoon
while I tramped alone through the Catoctin Mountains?
Light November snow swirled about my head
as I peered through tiny Japanese binoculars
at a crowned sparrow jumping
through the raspberry brambles.
Never crossed my mind
that a mother of four boys would worry,
whose only question would be, "Is he bleeding?"
And never crossed my mind that she would wonder why
I would walk for hours across the crunchy ground
interrupted only by summer weeds
sticking up through the snow,
getting my boot stuck
in the slender crevice of a rock outcropping
seemingly hiding secret caves and fox dens,
following those forsaken stone walls
built by long departed farmers who staked their claims
to the ridge that rimmed the valley.
All the while I missed her not hugging me and saying,
"You'll be okay,"
while I slogged and slipped up an icy knoll,
not knowing that's what it was all about.

A Quiet House: Before and After

Depression's dry dust would drift about the house
catching the back of my throat,
smothering any ability to weep my fate.
During the desert of a strain-full night
every switched-through cable channel
would seem tinny and distant.
The soft porn movies left the acrid taste
of making love to someone you really don't like.
Commercial breaks of steak knives and
saving lives from suicide made no impression.
No answer for the abiding question,
where and what's *my* stake in a new life?

Here I am now in my reborn state.
While my wife sleeps her peaceful dream,
how restful and reflective the night-full living room,
each chair, table, and piece of bric-a-brac
exudes the glow of a Christmas punch bowl.
Paterfamilias sips a glass of port
as porch chimes gentle a new day
and visiting grandchildren recharge
in their makeshift beds,
breathing in-and-out enough love
to jump up and down on the sofa in the morning,
waking grandfather who fell asleep
with the trace of a smile across his face.

About the Author

Robert Edward Miss, a native of Frederick, Maryland, has pursued a career in media, philanthropy, and the arts. But his life's passion has been poetry and storytelling. His first volume of poetry, *Fever Dreams: A Selection of Poetry,* is available on Amazon Kindle. His poetry has appeared in the *Crosswinds Poetry Journal, Austin International Poetry Festival, Spirit of Woman in the Moon, Writing the Walls of the Hudson Valley MOCA, The Lamp,* and *America.* He has received recognition from the Arvon International Poetry Award. Robert earned an AB degree from Fordham University in classics and philosophy and an MA from the UNC-Chapel Hill School of Media and Communications. As a boy, Rob Miss fished on the Monocacy and Potomac rivers and roamed the Appalachian Mountains. Those early experiences are reflected in many of his poems. Rob volunteered for more than a decade at gallery265, an arts program featuring artists with disabilities. As a result, he created the Our Art Belongs! Inclusion Program and founded the Fund for Artists with Disabilities via New York Community Trust.

www.robertedwardmiss.com

www.ingramcontent.com/pod-product-compliance
Lightning Source LLC
Chambersburg PA
CBHW070335090426
42733CB00012B/2484